D0672053

LEAF
PEEPING

Discover the Seasonal Wonder of Fall Foliage

By Erin Vivid Riley

Cover Art by Leila Simon Hayes
Interior Illustrations by Liana Jegers

LEAF
PEEPING

CHRONICLE BOOKS

SAN FRANCISCO

POCKET NATURE SERIES

Text copyright © 2022 by **ERIN VIVID RILEY**.

Library of Congress Cataloging-in-Publication Data available.

ISBN 978-1-7972-1742-0

Manufactured in China.

MIX
Paper from
responsible sources
FSC™ C136333

Series concept and editing by **CLAIRE GILHULY**.
Series design by **LIZZIE VAUGHAN**.
Cover art by **LEILA SIMON HAYES**.
Interior illustrations by **LIANA JEGERS**.

Typeset in Albra, Benton Sans, Caslon.

10 9 8 7 6 5 4 3 2 1

Chronicle books and gifts are available at special quantity discounts to corporations, professional associations, literacy programs, and other organizations. For details and discount information, please contact our premiums department at corporatesales@chroniclebooks.com or at 1-800-759-0190.

Chronicle Books LLC
680 Second Street
San Francisco, California 94107
www.chroniclebooks.com

CONTENTS

October is the month of PAINTED LEAVES. Their RICH GLOW now flashes round the world. As fruits and leaves and the day itself acquire A BRIGHT TINT just before they fall, so the year near its setting. October is its SUNSET SKY; November the later twilight.

—Henry David Thoreau, *Autumnal Tints,* the *Atlantic*

O ne day in early September, I woke up before dawn to make the drive to a hot spring just northwest of Santa Fe, where I live. The small mineral pools, of which there are three, cascade down a hillside that faces west. And if you time things just right, you can catch the bluff across the way gradually illuminate from the rising sun.

Most of the Jemez Mountains, a volcanic range at the southernmost tip of the Rockies, is high-altitude desert forest—Douglas fir, ponderosa pine, and blue spruce fill its dense woods. But set within a grove of quaking aspens, the springs inhabit a swath of yellow in an otherwise green sea. I had hiked to them a handful of times, but never in the fall. This time, the once-dirt trail was gilded with fallen leaves. The surrounding aspens glowed from above, their buttery leaves flickering with each gust of wind, to the point where I couldn't tell what was leaf and what was light.

As I walked, I felt an overwhelming sense of gratitude to the trees, these living beings. All winter, spring, and summer, they have faithfully done their duty: collecting a reserve of sugar to carry them through winter, sheltering way-faring critters, and providing cover for newer saplings. Since spring, they have expended as much breath into the air as they can muster.

I thought about their roots, ready to slow down, having burrowed farther into the earth. I imagined their newly bare branches, at once grateful for levity and missing their depart-ing companions. And the leaves themselves, submitting to the slow letting-go, waiting in anticipation—for a gust of wind, a drop of rain, or nothing at all—to fall to the earth. If only all living things could, in their final moments, flutter in the wind and kiss the earth.

I soon realized that I had spent an hour thinking about this and little else.

When I finally reached the springs, they were barely visible. It was their sulfurous smell and heat that gave them away—the pools were otherwise concealed by fallen leaves. When I put my hand in the water, it was like discovering them for the first time. It didn't matter that I had missed the sunrise vista I had planned to see. I got what I was searching for along the way: a moment of wonder and escapism. A stretch of time when I wasn't thinking about my day-to-day, but of the Earth and her mysteries.

That's the thing about maintaining your attention on something particular (whether within nature or elsewhere): What could be just another backdrop to our lives is actually a whole other world to explore. With leaf peeping, I started paying attention, and before I knew it, I could identify the difference between a simple and compound deciduous leaf. Soon after, I could spot a maple from an oak from a birch. And not long after that,

I could tell what the late-summer heat and sparse rainfall would mean for fall color. I started becoming so familiar with types of leaf-turning trees and their seasonal tendencies that a well-timed hike turned into a mental exercise, one that took me out of my temporal reality and into a somewhat meditative state.

I am no expert in phytomorphology (the study of the external structure of plants, including leaves), and this is by no means a scientific guide. But I can speak to the simple joy that comes from slowing down and appreciating something wondrous—a feeling experienced less and less by the disillusioned, screen-reliant, nature-deprived lot of us. I hope this pocket guide serves as both an invitation to get outside and a handy companion on your future excursions. Through a series of light explainers, illustrative how-tos, and thoughtful exercises, we'll explore leaf peeping in all its natural-phenomena glory, from why leaves change color to what the cycle can teach us. But mostly, I'll share how to use this beloved pastime to pay attention.

TO PEEP OR NOT TO PEEP?

For as long as leaf peeping has been a pastime in the Western world, there has been a very vocal subset of autumn-loving folk who have disliked the term. The word *peeping* has been criticized as childish, unpleasant, and erroneous. I'm here to offer a compromise.

As both a noun and a verb, *peep* seems to have too many meanings in the English language. From "a feeble shrill sound" to "a first glimpse," its many noun definitions aren't a fit. And as a verb, it doesn't make much sense either. According to Merriam-Webster, *peep* as a verb can mean:

---

1 a : to peer through or as if through a crevice
   b : to look cautiously or slyly

---

2 : to begin to emerge from or as if from concealment : show slightly

If you, like me, think at first that No. 2 is apt—
what are changing leaves if not carotenoids and
anthocyanins outlasting fading chlorophyll that
once concealed them (we'll get to this later)—
then there is some accuracy in the term. But
this definition also ascribes the "peeping" to the
leaves, which counters the idea that leaf peeping
is an activity for us, the beholders. Then again,
the meanings that *do* attribute the doing to us
("peering through" and "looking cautiously or
slyly") aren't quite appropriate either.

Let's look at how the activity is referenced in
other cultures. In Japan, where there's an entire
vocabulary devoted to fall and the turning of
leaves, *momijigari* (紅葉狩) translates to "an
excursion to hunt for autumn leaves," while
kanpūkai (観楓会), used more often in the country's northernmost island of Hokkaido, denotes
"a get-together to enjoy the autumn foliage." In
Korean, *dan pung ku gyeong* (단풍 구경) means a
purposeful look at the changing colors of leaves.
In Chinese, *shangye* (赏叶) loosely translates to
the reward or appreciation of leaves. What all

these characterizations have in common is a recognition of worth. Even the use of the word *hunt*, or *gari*, in *momijigari* doesn't mean what we may think it does—in this context, it means "to appreciate."

While we'll refer to the pastime in its traditional form throughout this book, I'd like to plant the seed for a different noun-gerund, one that combines English's simplicity with the sensibility for appreciation noted in the translations above. Consider the verbs you can use to describe this activity: *looking* versus *seeing*. The difference lies in having passive versus active engagement with stimuli. In this book, I'll show you how to pay attention—how to see. So whether you count yourself as a first- or longtime leaf peeper—or never want to be referred to as such again—let this be your guide to leaf seeing.

AN ALMANAC

▶ **1010**
The Tale of Genji, considered the first novel, is published during Japan's Heian Era (794 to 1185 AD), and references an imperial celebration of autumn foliage.

▶ **1500S**
The use of the terms *spring* and *fall* to reference the seasons first appeared in the 16th century, in conjunction with each other, but were referred to in their longer forms, as *spring of the leaf* and *fall of the leaf*.

▶ **1862**
"The autumnal change of our woods has not made a deep impression on our own literature yet. October has hardly tinged our poetry," writes Henry David Thoreau, about the season's impact on American culture, in an essay for the *Atlantic*.

► **1966**
For the first time, the term *leaf peeper* appears in print in a column in the Vermont newspaper, the *Bennington Banner*.

► **1966**
Simon & Garfunkel lament the passage of time in the song *Leaves That Are Green:* "Once my heart was filled with love of a girl / I held her close, but she faded in the night / Like a poem I meant to write / And the leaves that are green turn to brown / And they wither with the wind / And they crumble in your hand."

► **2021**
#leafpeeping is tagged on more than 260,000 posts on Instagram.

THE ORIGINAL LEAF PEEPERS

L eaf peeping has long been of cultural importance in Asia, centuries before it was popularized in Western culture in the 1800s. The earliest written account of the activity appears in what's considered the very first novel, *The Tale of Genji*. Dating back a thousand years to Japan's Heian Era (794 to 1185 AD), the sprawling work of fiction was written by Murasaki Shikibu while she was a lady-in-waiting in the imperial court.

In a chapter titled "Wisps of Cloud," the protagonist, Genji, the son of a Japanese emperor, muses: "I should like to indulge in the pleasures of the seasons—the blossoms, the autumn leaves, the changing skies. People have long weighed the flowering woods in spring against the lovely hues of the autumn moors, and no one seems ever to have shown which one clearly deserves to be preferred." He deems both seasonal occurrences equal in spiritual value, for both represent condensed cycles of life and death. Earlier, in a chapter titled "The

Green Branch," he meets a former lover to try to win her back, but she remains unmoved. They exchange passages of poetry through the blinds of her window until dawn, when he bids his last goodbye. It's autumn, and Murasaki uses the falling leaves, clearness of sky, and birdsong to connote a sense of loss and acceptance.

The fall setting of Genji's heartbreak isn't dull and gloomy, but full of beauty, clarity, and light. An ineffable combination of feelings— sadness, surrender, appreciation—that's reflected in the season informs a central adage in Japanese culture: *mono no aware*. At its most literal, the phrase means "the pathos of things." More metaphorically, it denotes an awareness of the impermanence or transience of the material world, and the beauty in that realization. In particular, *aware* means a sense of wonder or awe, or "the ohh- or ah-ness of things," as it's often rendered. Notably, the word *aware* appears in the book more than a thousand times.

The thematic relationship between fall foli- age and *aware* has persisted in art and literature.

From this poem, by Fujiwara Sadaie (1162 to 1241), one of Japan's most notable poets:

As I look afar,
I see neither cherry trees,
Nor tinted leaves:
Only a modest hut on the shore,
In the twilight of an autumn eve.

To this passage from Pico Iyer's 2019 book *Autumn Light: Season of Fire and Farewells*, based on his return to Japan following the passing of his father-in-law:

Autumn poses the question we all have to live with: How to hold on to the things we love even though we know that we and they are dying. How to see the world as it is, yet find light within that truth.

The British philosopher Alan Watts, who studied under the Japanese scholar and author D.T. Suzuki, defines it more precisely: "When the moment evokes a more intense, nostalgic sadness, connected with autumn and the vanishing away of the world, it is called *aware*," he writes in *The Way of Zen*. "*Aware* is not quite grief and not quite nostalgia in the usual sense of longing for the return of a beloved past. *Aware* is the echo of what has passed and what was loved, giving them a resonance such as a great cathedral gives to a choir, so that they would be poorer without it." The phrase is often used alongside others, such as *mujo*, a Buddhist term for ephemerality, and *wabi-sabi*, which is an aesthetic sensibility focused on accepting the imperfections of things around us.

This isn't to say that we should all use our leaf-peeping excursions to confront the inevitability of life. But let this remind us that there is something intrinsically introspective about the activity.

FALL, LEAVES, FALL;
die, flowers, away;
Lengthen night
and shorten day;
EVERY LEAF SPEAKS BLISS TO ME
Fluttering from the
AUTUMN TREE.
I shall smile when
wreaths of snow
Blossom where the rose
should grow;
I SHALL SING WHEN night's decay
Ushers in a drearier day.

—Emily Brontë, *Fall, Leaves, Fall*

I.

WHY LEAVES CHANGE COLOR

There's something deeply reassuring about seasonal phenomena—that, even if we're not entirely sure why something happens, it still does, more or less at the same time of year, every year. While with the changing of leaves, there is a general consensus on the ecological process that is taking place, and why yellows and oranges burst into view, there still isn't a definitive understanding of why some leaves change to red, scarlet, or purple.

The ecological *how* is easy enough to understand. The turning, known as leaf senescence, is initiated by the shorter days, drop in temperature, and diffusing light caused by the sun's retreat into the opposite hemisphere. This makes it so leaves can't perform as much photosynthesis, the process by which chlorophyll—which gives them their green color in the warmer months—traps light and uses it to convert water and carbon dioxide into energy for the tree and oxygen for us.

What is usually a net-positive formula during spring and summer, when the plant produces more energy than it expends, turns into a zero-sum game come fall. The leaves spend more energy producing chlorophyll than they can contribute back to the tree. To protect its energy store, the tree begins to block the leaves' nutrient supply by creating a seal at the petiole, where the leaves' stems meet the tree's branches. As the leaves' nutrient supply wanes, their ability to create chlorophyll subsides, and the green coloration diminishes. It's at this point that other pigments, previously masked by the green of the chlorophyll, start to emerge.

There are three main compounds that contribute to the changing colors. All deciduous

trees contain carotenoids, a bright yellow-orange pigment (also present in egg yolks,
flamingos, corn, and daffodils), which appears
as the chlorophyll supply begins to wane. For
a time, carotenoids help protect the remaining
chlorophyll and support it in the making of
glucose, trees' prime fuel; but as the chlorophyll
dwindles so does the green hue it produces
in the leaves, which allows the carotenoids
to come into view, resulting in yellow-orange
foliage. Only a few deciduous trees, like maples
and white oaks, feature anthocyanins, which
are produced in late summer. Anthocyanins are
responsible for brilliant scarlet hues. Raspber-
ries, apples, and morning glories also contain
this pigment. Lastly, tannins, found in all
hardwoods and also prevalent in tea and grape
leaves, are a tart chemical compound created
during decomposition, causing the leaves to
brown and fall off.

The presence of the yellows and oranges
is a chemical side effect, but the ecological
reasons for scarlet hues from anthocyanins is
still very much a modern-day mystery. One

theory is that the red coloring helps protect the leaves from sun damage during their last stages of life, since red is better at reflecting ultraviolet light. (This comes from studies that have shown that low temperatures and bright conditions cause anthocyanin production to speed up.) Even so, this doesn't answer the question as to why trees would use so much energy to protect a dying leaf. Another theory is that red acts as a warning sign for insects that might eat or lay eggs on the leaves, alerting them to look for more nutrients or permanence elsewhere. (Studies have shown that aphids looking to lay eggs to hatch the following spring are significantly more likely to avoid red-leafed trees.) In their own brilliant end, are the leaves exerting influence on the trees' existing systems, or are they working to avert outside threats? The truth is there is no solid consensus.

In a day and age when we seem to exhaust a subject as soon as it's discovered, it can be hard to imagine that anything about the life cycle of something as ubiquitous as a deciduous tree is still a code that needs to be cracked. For now, we'll forgive these gaps in our knowledge and focus on what to make of what we do know.

WHAT AFFECTS COLOR

For an early start to the foliage season, deep colors, and a long turning period, there needs to be cool, sunny days, a good amount of summer rainfall, and little wind. Too-warm autumn weather can cause the tree to hold onto its chlorophyll longer, which can delay and dull a tree's colors. Cooler weather and plenty of sunshine encourage the production of anthocyanins, resulting in more red foliage. Wet conditions can delay the turning process but an extreme amount of rainfall can stress a tree and cause it to transition early. Strong winds can force a premature falling, before leaves even get a chance to turn.

Some trees love heat and drought, the right amount of which can extend a species'

ADAPTED TO THE LEAVES: COLOR MEANINGS

Although biologists don't know for certain the ecological reasons why leaves turn the colors that they do, if we consider how humans are wired, we can at least view it as a lucky byproduct of evolution. Unlike other mammals, humans and other primates have three light-sensing cone cells in our eyes instead of two; the additional cell allows us to see reds and oranges. The common explanation is that this adaptation made it possible for us to see ripened fruits and edible foliage. While this is a useful ability, let's just be grateful that our ancestors evolved enough to let us see sunsets, all seven colors in a rainbow, and turning maple leaves.

growing season and delay its turning. However, extreme heat and drought has the opposite effect, causing leaves to turn earlier and faster. When that happens, instead of an all-at-once burst of color, we're left with different groups of trees turning at various times throughout the season. In some cases, trees that are stressed can fail to reveal the other colored pigments in their leaves and turn from green straight to brown, skipping their fall colors altogether.

These influences—sun, rain, wind, and temperature—along with the mineral content of the soil, latitude, and plant heredity, have long determined the composition of coloration.

THE IMPACT OF CLIMATE CHANGE

Throughout history, trees—and thus foliage—have been affected by a number of factors, from non-native species and insects to changing weather patterns and climate. For centuries, huge American chestnut trees were found from

Maine down through the South, and in the fall they created a wave of buttery yellow up and down the coast. But, within the span of a few decades starting in the late 1800s, a fungus native to Asia wiped them out, and in their place other species, like oaks, hickories, and maples, took over. The swaths of gold that gilded the eastern seaboard soon turned into an assortment of crimsons and bronzes.

More recently, North America's ash trees, which are among our most dependable for beautiful fall color, have come under threat from yet another import: the emerald ash borer. First observed in 2002, the jewel-toned beetle has since been spotted in some three dozen states and several Canadian provinces. Its larvae feed on phloem, the trees' main arteries in charge of transporting nutrients, causing an interruption to the plants' circulation. Since its arrival, the borer has been responsible for the destruction of tens of millions of ash trees and the loss of their kaleidoscopic colors (a white ash will often show ambers, crimsons, and burgundies at the same time).

While it's too soon to say which species will take the ash's place, studies have found that, in place of ash or other tree seedlings germinating in the wake of the destruction, there were fast-growing shrubs like honeysuckle and multiflora rose. And the fewer the ash trees, the lower the rate of reproduction among them, creating even less barrier to invasive species. Such dynamics have affected not only the long-term health of our forests but also, in the short term, the length and depth of fall colors.

At the time that Henry David Thoreau was chronicling his autumnal musings in the mid-nineteenth century, he confidently ascribed timelines to seasonal transformations. "By the twenty-fifth of September, the Red Maples generally are beginning to be ripe," he wrote. Later, he afforded some room, but was just as precise: "Now too, the first of October, or later, the Elms are at the height of their autumnal beauty, great brownish-yellow masses, warm from their September oven, hanging over the highway." And then again: "By the sixth of October the leaves generally begin to fall, in successive showers, after frost or rain; but the principal leaf-harvest, the acme of the Fall, is commonly about the sixteenth." Less than a century later, this timing would start to change.

The turning season generally begins in late August in Alaska and the tundra of northern Canada; in some parts of the South, leaf turning can extend into late November. While the degree and duration of autumn color range from year to year, the season's onset has gradually delayed in the past few decades due to warmer, drier summers. A study conducted by Harvard, which examined leaf turning in Massachusetts' Harvard Forest from 1993 to 2010, predicted that, with current climate-change forecasts, the duration of the fall display there would increase about one day every decade. Ultimately, we can expect the senescence season to arrive later and last longer as the planet warms.

Just as our movement is being impacted by rising temperatures, so, too, is that of trees. A 2008 study found that hardwoods in Vermont, such as the sugar maple and American beech, had begun migrating both to higher elevations and higher latitudes, toward Canada. Ecologists examined forest plots at different elevation zones in the Green Mountains, comparing their composition from 1964 to 2004. Using aerial photographs and satellite imagery, they estimated that the lower limit of the narrow region where the northern hardwood and boreal forests meet had moved upslope by more than 200 feet [61 m] in some places, and that the upper limit had moved upward by nearly 400 feet [122 m]. This is an enormous jump, considering that most of the peaks in the Green Mountains are only around 4,000 feet [1,220 m] tall.

What had been taking place was a changing of the guard. Higher elevations are made up of boreal forest, composed mostly of coniferous species. These trees thrive at altitude and in cooler climes. But as the historical environment for that forest type warms, boreal species become more scarce in the area where they meet hardwoods. Resulting gaps in the canopy make room for hardwoods—trees more adapted to warmer temperatures—to settle and thrive. This, along with a series of other findings, led the team to theorize that climate change was causing this move.

As for climate change's likely effects, an atlas created by the Forest Service, which models the potential habitats for 125 tree species in the face of rising temperatures, expects many deciduous hardwoods to be significantly impacted. Sugar maples, for example, are expected to lose much of their Appalachian habitat before the end of this century even if carbon dioxide emissions are drastically reduced. If emissions continue at a high rate, the maples' U.S. populations will be concentrated mostly in northern New England and the uppermost stretches of the Midwest. While Southern trees might move northward to take their place, few of those species are able to produce the ruby-red hue sugar maples are known for. And of course, this theory of northwards migration (rather than extinction) hinges on the assumption that all the other elements necessary are in place in the sugar maples' new home, particularly the mineral content of the area's soil.

At a time when people may still choose to ignore climate change's visual cues, perhaps practical changes to a beloved pastime like leaf peeping will spur greater thought. Let every outing serve as a reminder to get outside and enjoy the crisp air, beautiful foliage, and changing seasons while they last, and do what we can to preserve the wonders of our world.

A DICTIONARY FOR MINDFUL LEAF PEEPING

There aren't enough words in the English language to convey the season's ineffable feelings and thoughts, so I came up with a few of my own, inspired by John Koenig's project, The Dictionary of Obscure Sorrows. Surely, some cultures must have words for these already, but for the rest of us, here's a fall-foliage-feels glossary:

► **EMPATREE**
An uncanny capacity to anthropomorphize a tree and see yourself in its autumnal transformation, so that the falling leaves take on a palpable feeling of loss or levity, of surrendering or shedding some part of yourself that might or might not be missed come winter.

► **FOREVERENTIAL**
A humbling realization that the leaves will glow bright regardless of whether we're around to appreciate them or not; this realization may shock us out of a daily dreamstate that measures

our surroundings by how they reflect upon us or how we project upon them.

▶ **LEAFRACTION**
The way soft autumn light diffuses through yellow leaves, as if it's refracting rather than reflecting.

▶ **REFLIAGE**
The sight of a lone tree whose fallen leaves carpet the ground in the same shape of its summer umbrage, like a shadow of color and light. It's as if the image of the tree has been transposed, with the branches taking on the appearance of roots and the fallen leaves, its lush canopy.

▶ **THERMALINGER**
The feeling of being temporarily cocooned in warmth while walking or driving through a dense canopy of leaves flush with color, akin to the cozy sensations we often associate with winter, such as lingering in bed under a thick blanket after the first night of snowfall.

▶ **THICKETINGLING**
The eerie sensation that fall is on its way—a sudden crispness to the air, lucidity to the sunlight, and vague stirring of expectation—that's soon confirmed by scattered bursts of color.

A GLORIOUS OCTOBER, all red and gold, with mellow mornings when the valleys were filled with delicate mists as if the SPIRIT OF AUTUMN had poured them in for the sun to drain—amethyst, pearl, silver, rose, and smoke-blue. The dews were so heavy that the fields glistened like cloth of silver and there were such heaps of RUSTLING LEAVES IN THE HOLLOWS of many-stemmed woods to run crisply through.

—L.M. Montgomery, *Anne of Green Gables*

II.

WHERE, WHEN, AND HOW TO LEAF PEEP

Before we get to the how, let's explore the where and when of leaf peeping. The variety of deciduous trees and their adaptability mean that you'll find brilliant pockets of color all across North America come autumn, but catching the most vibrant displays in both classic fall destinations and unlikely corners of the wilderness will require a bit of planning.

To start, we'll briefly look at our continent's geography as it relates to which hardwoods thrive where. Then we'll get into the complexities of timing, of which there are many. As for advice on when to hit "peak color," which is how leaf peepers refer to the short span of time when leaves are at their brightest, I'll leave that to the experts. There are plenty of resources that predict this, from an annual report by Great Smoky Mountains National Park to state-specific hotlines that begin to emerge across the internet around Labor Day. Using satellite weather data and on-the-ground tools, these projections are your best guide for taking advantage of the season each year.

After the basics, we'll get into the specifics of where to go with a guide that highlights the groves, trails, and drives worth experiencing in each region. Also included are beautiful places to sit, stare, and think, which you'll find under the category called Reflection Points.

WHERE

The majority of hardwood forests in North America are found in the eastern half of the United States, from the Midwest to the Northeast to the

South, but many also abound across the West, too. The continent's breadbasket of fall color, however, resides on the spine of the Appalachians, which travel about 2,000 miles [3,200 km] from the Canadian provinces of Newfoundland and Labrador down to central Alabama. The range lies within the Eastern Deciduous Forest, an ecosystem that's mostly composed of temperate woodland. This biome occurs within the same latitudinal band across the world, from western Europe to eastern Asia, where you'll find plenty of incredible leaf-peeping destinations, too.

Although the entire range is a hotbed of tree diversity, the stretch of the Southern Appalachians ranging from northeast Georgia to central Virginia contains more tree species than anywhere else in North America, the vast majority of which are deciduous. Its evolutionary history, along with the range's dynamic variations in climate, altitude, topography, and soil composition, is what makes it so distinct. Specifically, a combination of long, warm summers and plenty of rainfall—around 60 to

100 inches [152 to 245 cm] per year, which is second only to the Pacific Northwest—makes for conditions that allow broadleaf trees to thrive over conifers.

The main difference between broadleaf trees and conifers is the degree to which they create and rely on photosynthesis. The more sunlight and water, the more photosynthesizing, and the faster the rate of growth; thus, climates with a lot of sunlight and water are more favorable for hardwoods, allowing new growth to thrive and outcompete evergreens. Coniferous trees are more efficient at conserving water and photosynthesizing year-round, and therefore thrive in harsher, more extreme environments—including throughout much of the West, where long seasonal droughts and heavier mountain snowpacks are more common than in the East or South.

Forest Types That See Fall Color

▶ **EASTERN DECIDUOUS FOREST**

East of the Mississippi River, steady rainfall all year and humid, warm summers provide trees with a longer growing season. All together, the conditions make for the highest density of hardwoods in North America.

▶ **BOREAL**

Long, cold, dry winters and short, cool, wet summers discourage deciduous trees, with the exceptions of larches and aspens, our hardiest of hardwoods. This forest commands much of Canada and the northern and high-altitude mountainous regions in the U.S.

▶ **MONTANE**

Similar to boreal forests, this type's weather patterns and prevalence on high elevations make for abundant pine country, though western larches can be found here, too.

NORTHERN
MIXED

EASTERN DECIDUOUS

COASTAL PLAIN
MIXED EVERGREEN

▶ TEMPERATE RAINFOREST

This woodland flourishes along the upper Pacific Coast, from southern Alaska to Northern California. The area receives plenty of rainfall. However, summertime, a tree's growing season, actually coincides with drier and relatively cool temperatures, making it so that hardwoods don't do well, though alders and bigleaf maples manage.

▶ NORTHERN MIXED FOREST

Common in regions with four distinct seasons, this forest type usually occupies the transition band between lower deciduous forests and upper coniferous forests. More adaptable and less sensitive hardwoods like beech and maple flourish here.

▶ COASTAL PLAIN MIXED EVERGREEN FOREST

Along the Atlantic and Gulf coastal plains, where swamps, marshes, and streams make for sandy, low-nutrient soil, only the most water-impervious of deciduous trees survive, like beech, maple, yellow poplar, and oak.

▶ GREAT PLAINS GRASSLANDS

Spanning two Canadian provinces and five midwestern states, this biome is one of the last remaining temperate grasslands in the world. While mostly prairie, the region's cold, dry winters and hot, mildly wet summers encourage oaks, cottonwoods, maples, and hackberries.

Leaf Peeping Abroad

A trip to parts of Europe and East Asia in the fall can mean iconic sights shrouded in color. Venture to any of these destinations for a breathtaking fall foliage escape:

▶ CAIRNGORMS NATIONAL PARK, SCOTLAND

The golden birch and alder in this park at the heart of the Scottish highlands turn shortly after the late summer bloom of purple heather on the moorland.

▶ AMSTERDAM, THE NETHERLANDS

The magical sight of the city's amber-lined canals and streets makes up for autumn's all-too-early afternoon sunsets.

▶ **JIUZHAIGOU VALLEY, CHINA**

Visitors flock to this nature preserve in Sichuan Province to view its glacial lakes and wild pandas, but come fall, they come to see the valley cloaked in color.

▶ **ANY TEMPLE IN KYOTO, JAPAN**

You can't go wrong with a stroll through the maple-filled gardens at temples such as Tōfuku-ji, Daigo-ji, and Ginkaku-ji.

WHEN

Late September is officially when foliage season begins, but you don't have to wait until then to start to see fall colors, which begin as early as late August in some places. To tell whether leaf-peeping season is approaching or upon us, look to the trees on mountaintops. The higher the elevation, the lower the temperatures, and, generally speaking, the cooler the climate, the faster leaves turn. This also goes for latitude,

with chillier, northern regions often display-
ing color first. Weather, genetic variation,
and local conditions all contribute to the
timing of turning leaves. As far as variables
go, temperature and rainfall are often the
most influential, as they differ by elevation
and location and therefore range across any
given landscape. (Sunlight, for example, also
contributes to leaf turning and sees a signifi-
cant shortening in the fall, but this change is
consistent across most parts of the Northern
Hemisphere.)

Imagine it this way: Color spilling down
from mountaintops, across hillsides, and
into valleys, before emptying out at the coast,
where trees are usually the last to change.
While trees near the coast tend to turn late,
owing to the oceans' temperature-regulating
effect, those near inland waterways, from lakes
to wetlands, usually change earlier, due to the
stress of receiving a little too *much* moisture
(just another variable to consider!).

While general timing is easy enough
to determine using a mix of background

knowledge and up-to-date reports, the length of time that a tree, grove, forest, or region exhibits fall color depends on a variety of influences that are more difficult to calibrate. Some of the factors that will force early change will also contribute to a shortened window of color. These include stressors like heavy winds and pollution; the strain causes trees to tap out sooner than those in more stable environments. This is why trees along roadways and in urban centers tend to turn before their sheltered siblings.

Finally, timing is also influenced by the species of tree, and even genetic variations within a single species. As a general rule of thumb, just remember that northern regions, mountain peaks, urban centers, roadways, and wetlands will see color first, while southern areas, valleys, healthy and dense forests, and coastal areas will usually turn late, sometimes as far into the season as November.

SOME TREE STANDS TURN BEFORE OTHERS?

If temperature and sunlight are the main drivers of when trees start senescence, then why do we so often see only one or a few trees turning in an otherwise solid patch of green? It's because of genetic variation, between species but even between different individuals within the same species. In the case of a stand of aspens, which are clonal—meaning that the trees share a root system and are genetic duplicates of a single organism—autumn makes it easy to distinguish one stand from another. Just head to the Rocky Mountains and look up to see different patches of gold at different stages of gilding. This characteristic also makes it easy to spot any genetic aberrations within a stand, for one or a few trees at a different turning phase will be particularly visible among its uniform grove.

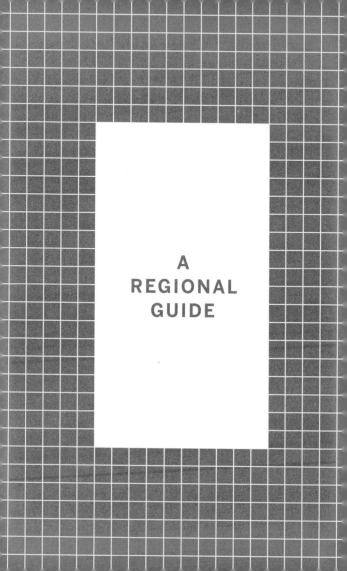

A
REGIONAL
GUIDE

NORTHEAST

When it comes to color displays, there are some places where the reds are richer, the oranges deeper, and the yellows brighter. The Northeast is one of them. Each of the region's states has its own special character come fall. When it comes to leaf peeping, Vermont, considered the country's foliage capital, cannot be missed. Forests cover more than three quarters of the state, and 71 percent of that woodland consists of maple, beech, and birch, promising non-stop splendor. Just east, in New Hampshire, the Lakes Region usually has one of the longest fall seasons—its 273 lakes are protected from the harsh winds of the coast and many don't rise more than 600 feet [183 m] above sea level. In Maine, the season will kick off in the inland mountains before ending at its craggy coast. Further south, coastal states such as New Jersey see fewer swaths of color, but the pockets that do turn, turn bright.

Leaf-Turning Trees

- ▶ Red and sugar maple
- ▶ American beech
- ▶ Yellow and paper birch
- ▶ White ash

The Forest

MOHAWK TRAIL STATE FOREST, MA

One of the state's largest remaining old-growth forest includes maples, birch, and ash.

The Trails

SUNSET RIDGE TRAIL, VT

6 mile [10.5 km] out-and-back, 2,687 foot [819 m] elevation gain

What starts in a canopy of maples, beeches, and birches quickly ascends above the treeline for unobstructed views of Lake Champlain poking through a color-drenched forest.

RICKETTS GLEN FALLS LOOP, PA

*7.2 mile [11.5 km] loop, 1,102 foot [336 m]
elevation gain*

A challenging hike that takes you past
21 waterfalls in Ricketts Glen State Park,
located where southern and northern hardwoods meet.

SOUTH TURNER MOUNTAIN, ME

*3.5 mile [5.6 km] out-and-back, 1,595 [486 m] foot
elevation gain*

The views from this peak are just as spectacular as its Baxter State Park siblings, including
the famed Mount Katahdin, but are reached
by a much shorter and easier trek.

FRANCONIA RIDGE LOOP, NH

*9 mile [14.5 km] loop, 3,480 foot [1,061 m]
elevation gain*

This ridgeline trail crosses three peaks in the
White Mountains and stays above the tree
line for more than a mile and a half.

MACEDONIA RIDGE TRAIL, CT
6.4 mile [10.2 km] loop, 1596 foot [486 m] elevation gain

A sea of sugar maples and ashes hug this route until the summit of Cobble Mountain, when they clear to reveal glorious sightlines to the Catskills and the Hudson River Valley.

The Drives

KANCAMAGUS HIGHWAY, NH
Conway to Lincoln, 36 miles [58 km]

This two-lane road cuts through the heart of White Mountain National Forest and ascends 2,855 feet [870 m] before reaching a series of breathtaking overlooks.

STOPS · C.L. GRAHAM OVERLOOK, SABBADAY FALLS

SCENIC ROUTE 1A, RI
Westerly to Wickford, 34 miles [55 km]

As you meander along the coast, you'll experience a calming contrast between changing leaves and beaches, inlets, and coves.

STOP · NINIGRET POND

MOHAWK TRAIL, MA

North Adams to Greenfield, 37 miles [60 km]

This stretch of old-growth oak trees was once a Native American trading footpath that connected the Hudson and Connecticut River Valleys.

STOP • HAIRPIN TURN AND LOOKOUT

THE SKIERS' HIGHWAY, ROUTE 100, VT

Stamford to Newport, 226 miles [364 km]

This pastoral country road passes by farms, streams, and covered bridges framed by the Green Mountains.

STOPS • LAKE WHITINGHAM, BUTTERMILK FALLS

The Reflection Points

PLANTING FIELDS ARBORETUM STATE HISTORIC PARK, NY

A 409-acre park filled with winding paths through gardens of golden larch, maples, and dogwoods that turn every color of the fall palette.

FALLINGWATER, PA

It's as if this house, a Frank Lloyd Wright masterpiece, was designed with autumn in mind. The cantilevered levels come framed in tulip poplars, red maples, and hickories, all reflected in the mountain stream that flows below the house.

HEIGHT OF LAND, ME

A small turnoff on Route 17 leads to a lookout over autumnal mountains reflected on five lakes, making for a surreal view of the landscape.

SOUTH

At the southern end of the Appalachian chain reside two of its most stunning ranges: the Blue Ridge Mountains, named for their bluish tint created by vapor that reflects the sky, and the Great Smoky Mountains, for the fog that cloaks their peaks and valleys. Come autumn, these two ranges are flush with every shade imaginable, and dotted with scenic vistas from which to take it all in. Along the coast in North and South Carolina, Georgia, and parts of Florida, the southeastern wetlands follow suit, turning gold and amber (though, due to the sandy composition of the soil, which causes water and nutrients to drain quickly, conifers tend to thrive here). Across inland plains, pockets of deep-purple dogwoods, glowing beeches, and marigold ash trees set the countryside alight.

Leaf-Turning Trees
- ▶ American beech and birch
- ▶ Mountain ash and maple
- ▶ Cherry
- ▶ Red oak

The Grove
ALBRIGHT GROVE, GREAT SMOKY MOUNTAINS
NATIONAL PARK, TN/NC

The tuliptrees, sugar maples, and eastern hemlocks in this plot make up some of the last-standing old-growth forest in the Appalachians. A short trail leads to a tuliptree that's 25 feet [7.6 m] in circumference.

The Trails
LITTLE RIVER FALLS, AL

0.75 mile [1.2 km] out-and-back, no elevation gain

This quick stroll off of Highway 35 brings you to a spectacular waterfall atop Lookout Mountain, where sassafras, dogwoods, hickories, and maples mingle.

BIG CREEK RIM TRAIL, TN

8.7 mile [14 km] loop, 1,574 foot [480 m] elevation gain
Start at the Great Stone Door overlook on
oak-dotted Cumberland Plateau, which kicks
off a series of color-packed lookouts on this
gradual hike.

WHITESIDE MOUNTAIN, NC

2.5 mile [4 km] loop, 511 foot [183 m] elevation gain
A cloudy day will bring the hazy tint that the
Blue Ridge Mountains are known for—and
a clear day will bring views as far as Georgia,
South Carolina, and Tennessee.

BEAR HAIR GAP TRAIL, GA

4.1 mile [6.5 km] loop, 928 [283 m] foot elevation gain
Streams and waterfalls fill this canopied route
that leads to oak-framed views of Lake Trah-
lyta in Vogel State Park.

BEAR ROCKS TRAIL, WV

*4.8 mile [7.7 km] out-and-back, 376 foot [115 m]
elevation gain*
The endpoint is a lookout on the windswept

plateau of Dolly Sods, where blueberry bushes that turn a bright crimson are contrasted with the yellows, oranges, and greens of Canaan Valley below.

The Drives

BLUE RIDGE PARKWAY, VA TO NC
Shenandoah National Park to Great Smoky Mountains National Park, 469 miles [755 km]
This route along the spine of the Blue Ridge, where the speed limit maxes out at 45 mph [73 kmh], forces you to slow down and take in more than 450 mileposts framed by dogwoods, sourwoods, and blackgums.

STOPS · BLOWING ROCK, RICHLAND BALSAM OVERLOOK, LINVILLE FALLS, CHIMNEY ROCK

SCENIC 7 BYWAY, AR
El Dorado to Jasper, 290 miles [467 km]
Traversing just about the entire state from north to south, through the Ouachita and Ozark National Forests, this drive is shrouded

in some of the most vibrant foliage the state has to offer.

STOPS · ROTARY ANN OVERLOOK, HOT SPRINGS NATIONAL PARK

LOOKOUT MOUNTAIN PARKWAY, TN TO AL

Chattanooga to Gadsden, 93 miles [150 km]

This roadway starts at its namesake, which towers above Chattanooga, before cutting through stands of some of Alabama's most colorful trees in Little River Canyon National Preserve.

STOPS · ROCK CITY GARDENS, RUBY FALLS

SKYLINE DRIVE, VA

Waynesboro to Front Royal, 105 miles [169 km]

Running the length of Shenandoah National Park before topping out at the Blue Ridges' crest, this route has views of the Shenandoah Valley to one side and Virginia's Piedmont region to the other.

STOPS · THE POINT OVERLOOK, MARY'S ROCK NORTH TRAIL

The Reflection Points

GIBBS GARDENS, GA

More than two hundred varieties of Japanese maples turn every autumnal color imaginable, from the amber of Sango Kakus to the burgundy of Bloodgoods.

MABRY MILL, VA

For a contemplative stop steeped in settler history, sit on the grassy banks overlooking this color-framed gristmill first built in 1905.

QUIET WALKWAYS, TN

It can be hard to find moments of calm at Great Smoky Mountains National Park, the country's most visited national park, but look out for these short, less crowded pathways, of which there are a dozen, for some one-on-one time with the area's fall color.

MIDWEST

Evergreens like hemlock and cedar pair with birches, maples, and poplars around the Upper Midwest. As you move south and west from the Great Lakes, dense forests of oak, poplar, basswood, and maple are interspersed with vast stretches of oak-dotted prairie, savanna, and farmland.

Leaf-Turning Trees
- ▶ Beech
- ▶ Birch
- ▶ Cottonwood
- ▶ Red and white oak
- ▶ Red and sugar maple

The Forest

WOLSFELD WOODS SCIENTIFIC AND
NATURAL AREA, MN

In the nineteenth century, homesteaders opted to establish a maple syruping operation when the area's topography proved too hilly to farm. Subsequently, some of the state's oldest sugar maples are found here.

The Trails

LEDGES TRAIL, OH

1.8 mile [2.9 km] loop, 80 foot [24 m] elevation gain

The sweeping views of Cuyahoga Valley National Park from this rocky outcropping are filled with sugar maples and white oaks.

RED TRAIL, WI

2.8 mile [4.5 km] out-and-back, 131 foot [40 m] elevation gain

Take turns between a white-sand lakeshore and honey-hued stretches of beech trees before ending up at Whitefish Dunes State Park's highest point, Old Baldy.

ESCARPMENT TRAIL, MI

8.4 mile [13.5 km] out-and-back, 1,666 foot [508 m] elevation gain

Known for its density of old-growth hardwood forests, the Porcupine Mountains light up in gold and bronze come fall.

OBERG MOUNTAIN LOOP, MN

2.3 mile [3.7 km] loop, 508 foot [155 m] elevation gain

The Superior National Forest, which sits at the transition zone between the state's northern boreal forests and southern deciduous areas, surrounds picture-perfect Oberg Lake and Lake Superior.

The Drives

TUNNEL OF TREES, MI

Petoskey to Cross Village, 20 miles [32 km]

Sunlight filters through an overhead canopy of maples and beeches that occasionally open up to reveal vistas of Lake Michigan.

STOP · THE BEACH AT MIDDLE VILLAGE PARK

ILLINOIS RIVER ROAD, IL
Ottawa to Havana, 150 miles [241 km]
Waterfalls, quaint towns, state parks, and some of the state's brightest trees are just a few of the highlights along this drive.

STOP · COUNCIL OVERHANG

COVERED BRIDGES SCENIC BYWAY, IA
Winterset to St. Charles, 82 miles [132 km]
This roadway served as the backdrop to the book and film *The Bridges of Madison County*, where the area's iconic overpasses are peppered across rolling landscapes of oaks and walnuts.

STOPS · PAMMEL STATE PARK, CLARK TOWER

The Reflection Points

BELLE ISLE CONSERVANCY, MI
There's something particularly calming about seeing Detroit across the river but feeling a world away. This Frederick Law Olmsted–designed island park is a unique wetland forest where oaks, elms, maples, and ash thrive.

ANDERSON JAPANESE GARDENS, IL

Built by master designer Hoichi Kurisu, this 12-acre conservatory is an oasis of koi ponds, waterfalls, and exotic hardwoods like Japanese maples and dogwoods.

MINNESOTA LANDSCAPE ARBORETUM, MN

This conservatory feels less like a garden and more like an organic forest, where bright-red sugar maples, burgundy dogwoods, and polychrome sumacs canopy the walkways.

MOUNTAIN WEST

In the Mountain West, where the landscape is dominated by the Rocky Mountains, it's all about elevation. The sudden shifts in altitude cause stark transitions between biomes—from cacti-filled deserts to high peaks of pines—but somewhere in between are deep canyons of multicolored sumacs, crimson maples, and lemon-yellow cottonwoods, as well as mountainsides of dense quaking aspens. Further north, in Montana and Idaho, grassy plains meet forested pockets of hardwoods.

Leaf-Turning Trees
- Aspen
- Larch
- Cottonwood
- Bigtooth maple
- Willow

The Grove

THE TREMBLING GIANT, UT

At this grove of quaking aspens, you can see the forest for the trees—the entire plot of some forty thousand trees is one organism, connected by a single root system that's estimated to be eighty thousand years old.

The Trails

ASPEN VISTA TRAIL, NM

12 mile [19.3 km] out-and-back, 2,480 foot [756 m] elevation gain

At the southern end of the Rockies, in the Sangre de Cristo Mountains, this steep trek at the base of Santa Fe's ski basin shimmers in gold against the area's green firs and spruces.

DYKE TRAIL, CO

13.7 mile [22 km] out-and-back, 2,334 foot [711 m] elevation gain

Home to the largest aspen forest in Colorado, Kebler Pass is blanketed with gold come fall, and this hike traverses the ridgeline that cuts through the heart of it.

WEST FORK TRAIL, AZ

7.8 mile [12.5 km] out-and-back, 728 foot [222 m] elevation gain

Follow a creek shrouded in oaks, cottonwoods, and bigtooth maples, which appear against a backdrop of towering red-rock cliffs in Coconino National Forest.

SCENIC OVERLOOK VIA BALD MOUNTAIN TRAIL, ID

3.5 mile [5.6 km] out-and-back, 951 foot [290 m] elevation gain

For a birds-eye view of the aspens and cotton-woods that blanket Sun Valley, head to the top of Bald Mountain.

The Drives

MILLION DOLLAR HIGHWAY, CO

Silverton to Ouray, 25 miles [40 km]

This crossing of the San Juan Mountains is packed with superlatives, from the summit of Red Mountain Pass to the depths of Uncompahgre Gorge, all of which burst into gold come fall.

STOP · BEAR CREEK FALLS OVERLOOK

ENCHANTED CIRCLE SCENIC BYWAY, NM

Taos to Eagle Nest, 84 miles [135 km]

Gold aspens and red cottonwoods light up a loop that passes by verdant Hondo Valley, the ancient pueblo of Taos, and the state's highest mountain, 13,161 foot [4,011 m] Wheeler Peak.

STOPS · RIO GRANDE GORGE BRIDGE, RED RIVER

LOGAN CANYON NATIONAL SCENIC BYWAY, UT

Logan to Garden City, 40 miles [64 km]

Known as the state's capital of fall color, Cache Valley's Norway maples, honey locusts, and elms erupt into scarlet, orange, and canary gold.

STOPS · UINTA-WASATCH-CACHE NATIONAL FOREST, BEAR LAKE

HIGHWAY 2, MT

Whitefish to St. Mary, 76 miles [122 km]

This larch-lined road traces the southern boundary of Glacier National Park, a less trafficked alternative to the park's famed Going-to-the-Sun Road.

STOP · TWO MEDICINE VALLEY TRAILS

The Reflection Points

FIFTH WATER HOT SPRINGS, UT

A cold waterfall meets a series of natural hot sulfur pools, which appear as if by magic in a dense forest of pines interspersed with oaks, maples, and alders.

DECISION POINT, MT

This overlook at the confluence of the Missouri and Marias Rivers, where Lewis and Clark spent ten days deciding which way to take, explodes in marigold come fall.

JOHN DENVER SANCTUARY, CO

This little enclave off of Aspen's Main Street honors the folk singer, activist, and state poet laureate with a colorful wetland display fed by the Roaring Fork River, which runs through it.

PACIFIC WEST

Sure, redwoods, Joshua trees, and Mexican fan palms are attractions in their own right, but the West has plenty of deciduous fall color if you know where to look. On the Pacific coast, you'll find oaks and maples in lower, wetter areas, like stream beds and canyons. In California, head north for displays across the Sierra Nevada, as well as on the north coast and in parks around the Bay Area. In the Pacific Northwest, the Columbia River Gorge lights up with big-leaf and vine maples and the Cascades with fiery aspens and larches, which are made even brighter against a backdrop of evergreens.

Leaf-Turning Trees

- ▶ Aspen
- ▶ Maple
- ▶ Oak
- ▶ Ash
- ▶ Larch

The Forest

THE ENCHANTMENTS, WA

This region within the Alpine Lakes Wilderness of the Cascades is known for its collection of western and subalpine larch groves that glow bright yellow against granite peaks.

The Trails

MOUNT MCLOUGHLIN TRAIL, OR

10 mile [16 km] out-and-back, 3,923 foot [1,196 m] elevation gain

The top of 9,495 foot [2,894 m] Mount McLoughlin provides an ideal vantage from which to watch groves of aspen leaves dancing.

BISHOP PASS TRAIL, CA

10 mile [16 km] out-and-back, 2,345 foot [715 m] elevation gain

Start at aspen-ringed South Lake before ascending into a patchwork valley between the Inconsolable Range and Hurd Peak.

COLCHUCK LAKE TRAIL, WA

8 mile [13 km] out-and-back, 2,280 foot [695] elevation gain

Larches gild this beautiful stretch of the Enchantments.

The Drives

HIGHWAY 2, WA

Blewett Pass to Lake Wenatchee, 48 miles [77 km]

From Blewett Pass, head to the maple-filled town of Leavenworth before cutting through lush Tumwater Canyon and ending at larch-lined Lake Wenatchee.

STOP · WATERFRONT PARK

MCKENZIE PASS, OR

Eugene to Sisters, 95 miles [153 km]

A drive from the Willamette Valley to the east of the Cascades takes you from electric-yellow black walnuts in urban Eugene to the scarlet-red vine maples near the pass's black lava fields.

STOPS • DEE WRIGHT OBSERVATORY, CASTLE ROCK TRAIL

JUNE LAKE LOOP, CA

June Lake Junction, 15 miles [24 km]

Circle around four bright-blue lakes that reflect crimson and gold splashes of cottonwoods, aspens, and willows against a backdrop of big-toothed peaks in the eastern Sierra.

STOPS • JUNE LAKE OVERLOOK, RUSH CREEK TRAIL

The Reflection Points

WASHINGTON PARK ARBORETUM, WA

This stop is filled with rare deciduous transplants such as fragrant witch hazels, multicolored black gums, and electric mountain ashes, plus one of North America's largest collections of Japanese maples.

SILVER FALLS STATE PARK, OR

A short stroll brings you to an overlook at the top of a 177 foot [54 m] waterfall surrounded by yellow maples.

CROOKED BUSH
(SASKATCHEWAN)

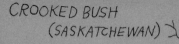

THE ENCHANTMENTS (WA)

BISHOP PASS
TRAIL
(CA)

GLACIER
NATIONAL PAR
(M

RIO GRANDE
GORGE BRIDGE
(NM)

LEAF-PEEPING SIGHTS

NOTRE-DAME-
DES-NEIGES
(QUÉBEC)

BELLE ISLE
CONSERVATORY (MI)

ANDERSON
JAPANESE
GARDENS (IL)

FRANK LLOYD
WRIGHT'S
FALLING WATER
(PA)

MABRY
MILL (VA)

CANADA

Much of Canada falls within the boreal-forest belt that rings around the globe across Alaska and much of Scandinavia, Siberia, and Russia. Its swaths of temperate and transitional forest are primarily found in its Atlantic provinces of New Brunswick, Nova Scotia, Prince Edward Island, and Newfoundland and Labrador, where you'll find the same variety and depth of color as in the Northeastern United States—just without the crowds. These forest types extend into Québec and Ontario. Also, similar to in the States, as you travel west, aspens, larches, and birches take the place of maples, ashes, and elms.

The Groves and Forests

HUMBER VALLEY, NEWFOUNDLAND AND LABRADOR
Located on the Humber River at the base of the Appalachian Mountains' nothern terminus, this valley bursts into a color medley thanks to its many maple trees.

MANITOULIN ISLAND, ONTARIO
This isle in Lake Huron is so dense with hardwoods and lacking in development that stepping onto it feels more like entering your own personal woodland than a sprawling park.

THE CROOKED BUSH, SASKATCHEWAN
Due to a unique genetic anomaly, the aspens in this grove don't grow straight. Instead, they twist and turn in every direction, giving off an eerie, otherworldly effect.

The Trails

MISCOU ISLAND PEAT BOG TRAIL, NEW BRUNSWICK
0.5 mile [0.8 km] loop, no elevation gain
Almost half of this island's acreage consists of peat bogs covered in various species of

blueberry bushes, which turn a stunning scarlet for a brief window come fall.

CAP BON AMI, QUÉBEC

2.8 mile [4.5 km] out-and-back, 930 foot [283 m] elevation gain

This popular trail in Forillon National Park cuts through a thicket of maples before arriving at a cliffside lookout, from where you can often see dolphins and seals.

LARCH VALLEY TRAIL, ALBERTA

6.9 mile [11 km] out-and-back, 2,621 foot [799 m] elevation gain

Starting at Moraine Lake in Banff National Park, this hike cuts through the Valley of Ten Peaks' golden-larch forest and tops off at Sentinel Pass.

The Drives

CABOT TRAIL, NOVA SCOTIA

Baddeck to Chéticamp, 186 miles [298 km]

On this leg of the Cabot Trail loop, wind through a lush forest of sugar maples, birches, and American beeches in the Cape Breton Highlands, a plateau ringed by towering cliffs that drop into the Atlantic.

STOPS • INGONISH BEACH, SKYLINE TRAIL

THE FUNDY TRAIL PARKWAY, NEW BRUNSWICK
Alma to Fundy National Park, 19 miles [30 km]
Despite the short mileage, you'd be hard-pressed to fit this drive into a day: trails, rivers, beaches, fishing villages, and two UNESCO designated sites dot this color-packed parkway.

STOPS • FUNDY FOOTPATH, FUNDY BIOSPHERE RESERVE, STONEHAMMER GEOPARK

NIAGARA RIVER PARKWAY, ONTARIO
Fort Erie to Niagara-on-the-Lake, 34 miles [56 km]
Winston Churchill called this "the prettiest Sunday afternoon drive in the world" for its river-hugging road, dramatic gorges, and eponymous waterfall, made all the better in autumn by the area's turning maples.

STOPS • BUTTERFLY CONSERVATORY, NIAGARA PARKS BOTANICAL GARDENS

The Reflection Points

JENNIEX HOUSE, NEWFOUNDLAND
AND LABRADOR

Behind this historic saltbox-house-turned-museum are two benches that watch over Bonne Bay and the Tablelands, a unique geological formation that looks like a patch of desert in the otherwise leafy Gros Morne National Park.

SANDBANKS PROVINCIAL PARK, ONTARIO

Spend an afternoon relaxing on a sand dune that overlooks sugar maple–lined Lake Ontario. The park is circled by the largest freshwater barrier beach in the world.

NOTRE-DAME-DES-NEIGES, QUÉBEC

This resting place is also an arboretum with more than 13,000 rare and old-growth trees, many of which have been standing for more than a century.

MAKE THE MOST OF YOUR SENSES

When most of us think of fall foliage, we don't just picture the colors of the forest—we imagine the satisfying crunch of leaves underfoot, the gentle rustling of branches overhead, and the scent of earth wafting up around us. Add a little focus, or mindfulness, to these sensations as you're walking in a forest, and you'll be surprised at just how meditative leaf peeping can be.

▶ **TOUCH**

Imagine the wind that's passing through the canopy above is also passing through you, taking with it the parts of you you're ready to let go of, as it will eventually do with the tree's turning leaves. Allow this to take on a cleansing effect. Feel the wind dance across your skin, the cool air caress your cheek. Let the breeze wash over you in the same way you would allow the sea to gently move your body underwater.

► **SOUND**
While you're walking on a forest floor laden with leaves, imagine that every gentle crunch underfoot is keeping you in rhythm with your surroundings. Make each step feel deliberate. You're setting your own pace and getting lost in your body's cadence. In the same way that *ujjayi*, the most common breath-control techniques in yoga, makes a simple bodily function audible and therefore more tangible, let the sounds of your physical movement help you focus.

► **SMELL**
Scent is the sense most closely linked to our memory and emotions, so it's fair to assume we're all likely to engage with it differently. There are some people who experience a particular aroma come fall; they describe it as either a feeling (melancholy is common) or as something more material, usually of dirt or dust. When leaves pass and fall, they release gases that can sometimes smell like chlorine or a dryer vent; when they decompose, they emit an earthy musk. If this scent incites any sadness for you, create a new memory association by seeking out a katsura tree. Its fallen leaves, especially when crumpled by hand, smell like caramel, vanilla pudding, or cotton candy.

► **TASTE**

The brighter the fall colors, the healthier the forest, and the sweeter the air tastes. Show gratitude for soon-to-fall leaves by being more conscious of your breathing, for the leaflets have spent all summer taking in carbon dioxide to give you oxygen. Let their hard work fill your lungs before the temperature drops and the air thins.

► **SIGHT**

Each vantage point provides its own special moment for contemplation. Looking up from under the canopy, notice the way color moves across the leaves themselves and the tree as a whole. In a leaf, pigment usually appears at the edges first before moving inward toward its veins and stem. In a tree, color typically begins at its top before spilling over its sides and closing in on its interior. This retreat of green suggests that a tree's source of life isn't gone, but is simply in hiding. Let this be a reminder that all that is lost is not gone forever. Finally, looking out above the canopy from above, observe how the patchwork of individual trees and groves creates a scene that's more beautiful in its variation than its uniformity.

O hushed
October morning mild,
THY LEAVES HAVE RIPENED TO THE FALL;
Tomorrow's wind, if it be
wild,
Should waste them all.
The crows above
the forest call;
Tomorrow they may form
and go.
O hushed
October morning mild,
Begin the hours
of this day slow.

—**Robert Frost,** excerpt from "October"

III.

FOLIAGE OF NOTE

We would need another entire guidebook to be able to include all the trees and shrubs in North America that change color. In this section, you'll find an overview of the most prevalent and vibrant trees to seek out. For the most part, each tree type has a few commonly found species that are known for bright displays—while leaf shape, size, and characteristics may vary, we'll stick to generalizations. The overstory, which comprises the layer of foliage at the top of the forest canopy, usually gets all the fall glory, but it doesn't mean we should overlook the smaller trees, shrubs, and vines—found in the understory section—that exhibit their fair share of color.

THE OVERSTORY

ASH

Common Species	White, green, and mountain
Leaf Look	All share the same oblong leaf shape; whites and mountains transition from a burnt yellow to a deep burgundy; greens stick to a brilliant yellow
Characteristics	Impatient, turning and shedding its foliage early
Reach	A range that spans north to south, east of the Mississippi River
Average Lifetime	120 to 300 leaf cycles

ASPEN

Common Species	Quaking and bigtooth
Leaf Look	Circular coins of canary yellow that tremble in the breeze
Characteristics	Shy but curious, found fluttering in groves on mountain slopes and often seeking out refuges inside canyons and along creeks; intrepid, taking over burned areas and other disturbed sites
Reach	Across North America from 5,000 to 12,000 feet [1,524 to 3,658 m] in elevation. Generally, the higher the latitude, the lower the elevation, and vice versa.
Average Lifetime	50 to 150 leaf cycles

BEECH

Common Species	American
Leaf Look	Oblong, tooth-edged leaves that permeate color from its veins, from dijon-yellow to bronze
Characteristics	Enduring, taking its time to turn, starting late and even keeping hold of its browned leaves deep into winter
Reach	From Nova Scotia west to Ontario, down through Wisconsin, and south to eastern Texas and northern Florida
Average Lifetime	150 to 400 leaf cycles

BIRCH

Common Species	Paper, black, yellow, river, cherry
Leaf Look	Variations of yellow, from cool lemon to warm honey, appearing on ovate leaves against a silvery or black bark
Characteristics	Optimistic, with thin, effervescent leaves that radiate light even on overcast days
Reach	A hardy tree; papers are found in cooler and moist areas across the east; yellows, blacks, and cherries are found more upland and along rivers from New England to the Gulf Coast
Average Lifetime	40 to 300 leaf cycles

CHERRY

Common Species	Black and pin
Leaf Look	Narrow leaf clusters that range from butter-yellow to creamsicle in a black cherry, and go purplish-red in a pin
Characteristics	Benevolent, with its wood, bark, and spring fruit providing multiple uses, from cough medicine to wine
Reach	These oval-shaped trees are found in southeastern Canada and throughout the eastern U.S.
Average Lifetime	50 to 100 leaf cycles

COTTONWOOD

Common Species	Eastern, black, and Fremont
Leaf Look	A rich mustard blankets the heart-shaped, ridged leaves of healthy trees, while burnt yellow is more common on those that are stressed
Characteristics	Dependable, often used as ornamental trees for their fast growth rate and ability to withstand drought conditions
Reach	While the eastern cottonwood can be found all over the Northeast, the black and Fremont occur in and around the Rocky Mountains and Pacific Coast
Average Lifetime	100 to 200 leaf cycles

ELM

Common Species	American, rock, and slippery
Leaf Look	Serrated-edge leaves that turn a warm saffron, often holding onto splashes of green
Characteristics	Stately and solitary, with a commanding wide shape and a tendency to stand alone
Foliage Reach	With great variety in environment between species, American elms thrive in open areas all over eastern North America, rock elms in wet uplands from Québec to Florida, and slippery elms in east-central Canada and the Midwest
Average Lifetime	175 to 200 leaf cycles

HICKORY

Common Species	Shagbark, shellbark, and mockernut
Leaf Look	Leaves that increase in size as they move up the stem go bronze to Tuscan yellow.
Characteristics	Resilient, often managing well in drought-like conditions that cause the edges of its leaves to brown
Reach	Drier hillsides and bluffs, from the Great Lakes and Great Plains to the Gulf Coast
Average Lifetime	200 leaf cycles

LARCH

Common Species	Western and subalpine
Leaf Look	Conifer-like needles that burst into gold and shed come fall
Characteristics	Cheeky and elusive, turning quick and bright across very specific elevations
Reach	Located primarily in the Pacific Northwest, with western larches typically found between 1,600 to 7,000 feet [488 to 2,134 m] and subalpines above 5,200 feet [1,585 m]
Average Lifetime	600 to 800 leaf cycles

MAPLE

Common Species	Red and sugar
Leaf Look	A three- to five-fingered leaf that's usually the first to turn and one of a few to last until winter; scarlet for red maples and a sunset spectrum for sugars
Characteristics	Easygoing and adaptable, able to grow in various conditions; generous, providing its sap every spring
Reach	The most common deciduous trees in the Northeast, flourishing from southern Canada down to the Gulf (for reds) and southern Appalachia (for sugars)
Average Lifetime	100 to 300 leaf cycles

OAK

Common Species	Red and white
Leaf Look	Long-lasting hues that range from a deep rhubarb to cherry-red on ornamental leaves in red oaks; slow-to-reveal shades of rosé and orange on shallow-lobed leaves in white oaks
Characteristics	Particular, preferring a diet of well-balanced soil and plenty of sunlight
Reach	These valuable trees can be found from the Midwest and the South to the Atlantic coast, as well as in drier pockets of the Pacific Northwest
Average Lifetime	200 to 300 leaf cycles

SASSAFRAS

Common Species	Only one in genus
Leaf Look	Adorable mitten-shaped leaves (sometimes with three lobes) that see every color of the fall spectrum
Characteristics	Opportunistic, seeking out clear-cut areas, from roadways to hiking trails
Reach	These distinct trees stretch from southern Canada to central Florida, east of the Mississippi River
Average Lifetime	100 leaf cycles

SOURWOOD

Common Species	Only one in genus
Leaf Look	Long oblong leaves go deep berry-red, sometimes with tinges of yellow
Characteristics	Stubborn, holding its intensity of color late into the season
Reach	These native trees can be found from southern Appalachia out to the Atlantic Coast
Average Lifetime	100 to 200 leaf cycles

TULIP

Common Species	Only one in genus
Leaf Look	Grand, broad trunks lead to a canopy of tulip-shaped leaves that range from rust to gold
Characteristics	Protective and proud, keeping watch over mixed forests from a height of up to 200 feet [61 m]
Reach	Usually one of few in a forest, though found across the Northeast in nutrient-rich and well-drained areas
Average Lifetime	200 to 250 leaf cycles

Blueberries *fig. 1*
Lowland blueberry shrubs are responsible
for intense displays of bright tangerine and
crimson that blanket rolling meadows, wetlands, and hillsides along the Atlantic, Pacific,
and Gulf Coasts, along with the Great Lakes
region.

Flowering Dogwood *fig. 2*
Native to most of the eastern United States
and southern Ontario, and usually found
beneath oaks and sassafras, this small tree
turns its branches up during fall as if reaching
for the sky. Its leaves range from wine-red to
light orange.

Juneberries *fig. 3*
These small hardwoods, also called shadbush,
often contain multiple hues of berry and

apricot on a single leaf, causing the entire tree to look like it's on fire.

Sumac   *fig. 4*
Though this tropical-looking plant is con- sidered a weed, it's palm-like leaves that turn a prismatic mix of amber and imperial red are so distinct from other hardwoods that it's worth keeping an eye out for. Especially because they usually grow in areas we're likely to encounter, from roadsides and trails to forest boundaries.

Virginia Creeper   *fig. 5*
It's a sight to see the bright scarlet leaves of this spirited vine against a tree trunk or forest floor. They usually turn before trees, making the display all the more startling.

THE EXCEPTIONS TO THE RULE:
DECIDUOUS CONIFERS

A long with larches (which are often called tamaracks—same tendencies, different species and growing location), there are a few other conifers whose needles change color and shed every fall. The second most common, bald cypress trees, take us from the high-alpine environment of larches and tamaracks to the swamps found in the Mississippi Valley, the Gulf Coast, and much of the southern Atlantic coast. Come fall, they turn shades of yellow, cider, and ruby—a beautiful contrast against the muted wetlands they inhabit and the water they often grow from.

The dawn redwood, with a grandeur that rivals the beloved Pacific redwood, has fern-like foliage that takes on a copper-orange hue. It glows especially bright due to the way the sun disperses through its canopy. This dinosaur-era species was widespread in North America during the Tertiary Period (about

66 million to 2.6 million years ago) and was thought to have gone extinct until a forester discovered one in the Sichuan province of China in 1944. Since then, it's been planted all over the world, including in various botanical gardens in the U.S. For the best showing, head to Crescent Ridge Dawn Redwoods Preserve in North Carolina, where there are around two hundred dawn redwoods.

DECISION TREE: A NOT-SO-SCIENTIFIC GUIDE TO LEAF IDENTIFICATION

When it comes to identifying hardwoods by their leaves, the only golden rule is that there is always an exception to the rule. Use this sequence to narrow down the possibilities by studying the leaf's structure.

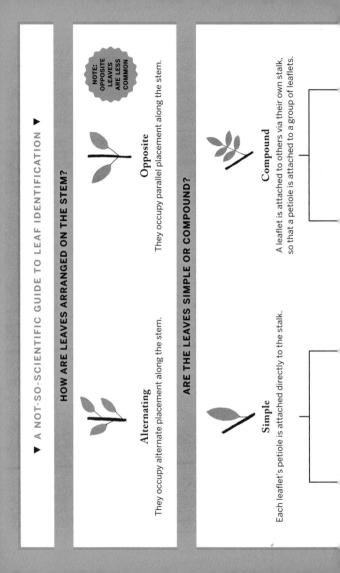

▶ A NOT-SO-SCIENTIFIC GUIDE TO LEAF IDENTIFICATION ▶

HOW ARE LEAVES ARRANGED ON THE STEM?

Alternating

They occupy alternate placement along the stem.

Opposite

They occupy parallel placement along the stem.

NOTE: OPPOSITE LEAVES ARE LESS COMMON

ARE THE LEAVES SIMPLE OR COMPOUND?

Simple

Each leaflet's petiole is attached directly to the stalk.

Compound

A leaflet is attached to others via their own stalk, so that a petiole is attached to a group of leaflets.

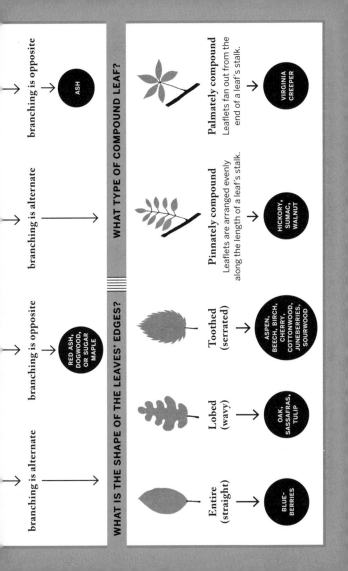

branching is alternate → branching is opposite → | branching is alternate → branching is opposite → **ASH**

branching is opposite → **RED ASH, DOGWOOD, OR SUGAR MAPLE**

WHAT TYPE OF COMPOUND LEAF?

Palmately compound
Leaflets fan out from the end of a leaf's stalk.

→ **VIRGINIA CREEPER**

Pinnately compound
Leaflets are arranged evenly along the length of a leaf's stalk.

→ **HICKORY, SUMAC, WALNUT**

WHAT IS THE SHAPE OF THE LEAVES' EDGES?

Toothed (serrated)

→ **ASPEN, BEECH, BIRCH, CHERRY, COTTONWOOD, JUNEBERRIES, SOURWOOD**

Lobed (wavy)

→ **OAK, SASSAFRAS, TULIP**

Entire (straight)

→ **BLUE-BERRIES**

A LEAF-PEEPING MEDITATION

The next time you venture out on a leaf-peeping excursion, search for a quiet spot to sit. Perhaps there's a cool stone or boulder, a fallen tree trunk, or simply a patch of mossy ground to relax on. Get comfortable. Let your sit bones connect to the earth, your brow unfurrow, your jaw go slack. Look up or out at the trees in front of you. Perhaps you'll use this pocket guide to identify the trees in a moment, but for now, just look. What do you see? What colors are on display—gold, amber, rust, burgundy? Take note of them, remembering that the forest puts on this show every year. Not for us, not for anyone, just because. We are simply lucky bystanders to this grand spectacle. Remember, too, that most leaves shine bright until their end, giving all they have until the moment they break away and fall to the dirt. And rest easy knowing that come spring, new life and leaves will take their place.

Once your mind is calm and quiet, you can choose to meditate on or journal about one of the following topics; jot down some field notes about your surroundings; or simply observe, appreciate, and enjoy.

1. *What colors draw your eye the most? Do you notice more variation, more detail the longer you sit?*

2. *What can we learn from this unsolicited display of beauty?*

3. *What can we appreciate in this unending cycle of regeneration?*

4. *How do you feel when you're in nature— restored, empowered, insignificant? How can you let this feeling inform other parts of your life?*

5. *Write a letter of gratitude to the trees and their leaves for giving us oxygen, for sharing their beauty, and for all their work since spring.*

And all the lives
we ever lived and
all the lives to be
are <u>FULL OF TREES</u>
and <u>CHANGING LEAVES</u> ...

—Virginia Woolf, *To the Lighthouse*

IV.

WHAT WE CAN LEARN FROM THE CYCLE

everal years ago, I spent all day at an
Agnes Martin retrospective at the
Guggenheim in New York. Those who
have visited will know that the museum is
essentially a hollow cylinder. Inside, its main
exhibition space is a long walkway that spirals
up along its outer walls, so that the more you
ascend, the more you see. You can gauge the
entirety of the exhibition from any given point,
and since it's one way, you have to return
from whence you came. This makes for a very
unique viewing experience, one that allows for
some personalization. On that particular day,
because I was free until the museum closed
and because it was Agnes Martin, an artist I

love but whose works I'd rarely seen in person, my plan involved lingering at every stop, occasionally looking out to see how a just-visited or soon-to-be-visited piece appeared from a distance.

This made for a few lasting impressions. Only after spending a few minutes in front of one of the dozen pieces that comprise "The Islands I-XII" (1979) did I see underlying shades of purple and blue in what otherwise would have seemed like variations of off-white. Pausing for long enough to truly focus on the work allowed me to uncover new details I hadn't seen before. Despite my plan, I found that the pieces I enjoyed most on my way up weren't the same on the way down. And because the show was arranged chronologically, the gradual progression of her work hit differently in each direction.

There are few environments that encourage, let alone allow space for, this kind of stopping and staring, a practice that's crucial for seeing. Art and nature can be two exceptions. For anyone who has spent time looking at a piece in a gallery or museum, you'll know that there's often a direct correlation between the length of time you spend looking at something and how much you're able to take from it. The same can be said for leaf peeping. Luckily, with a little practice, we can pay attention to and appreciate that which is fleeting (the Agnes Martin show ran from October to January, a period that's a month longer than your typical fall foliage season). Directing your attention is the easy part—it's the holding of it that requires practice.

I thought of this during a fall morning hike on the Aspen Vista Trail, which cuts through Santa Fe's beloved aspen groves. As I climbed, I let myself linger and occasionally stop to study the golden leaves. I noticed the patterns—which tree's leaves were at a similar stage of turning and therefore likely part of the same stand; the depth of color increasing as I gained elevation. I focused on immediacy as I climbed, on how the leaves appeared from below the canopy, knowing that the descent would be filled with vantage points from which I could take in longer sightlines. As with other sights in nature—and in art and daily life—there was a lot to see when I made a conscious effort to see it.

Now that we have a deeper understanding of leaf senescence and the wonders of foliage, let's explore what other lessons we can take away from the cycle, which mainly constitute rebukes of modern-day priorities.

FORGET #FOMO

If seeing your social media feed fill up with pretty pictures of foliage incites fear that you've already missed out on the leaf peeping window—fear not. As far as natural phenomena go, fall color is one of the most forgiving. Unlike solar eclipses and meteor showers, the changing of leaves is reliable and enduring, providing a grace period for those of us who like to experience the world at our own pace. It's also democratic in its convenience. It's widespread and relatively long-lasting. If you want to have it to yourself, hike into the backcountry or kayak along the edge of a lake, but you can just as easily take it in from a car window or on a walk around the neighborhood. To see just how accessible autumn foliage is in relation to other natural phenomena, consult the chart on page 120 for a brief ranking.

LET THE LEAVES FALL WHERE THEY MAY

Not only do fallen leaves act as rich topsoil for new-growth trees in spring, but they provide essential food, shelter, and nesting material for all kinds of wildlife. Birds use leaf litter to hide a winter's supply of nuts and acorns, squirrels and chipmunks use fallen leaves as insulation for their burrows, and butterflies and moths hibernate in them throughout winter. Leaves have life within them even after they die, a reminder that things that appear inanimate are often thrumming with unseen purpose.

HOW ACCESSIBLE AUTUMN FOLIAGE IS IN RELATION TO OTHER NATURAL PHENOMENA

Accessibility	Phenomena	Frequency	Duration	Location
1	Fall foliage	Once a year	3 months	Across North America, Europe, South America, Asia
2	Bioluminescent bays	Year-round	All night	Puerto Rico
3	Perseids meteor shower	Once a year	1 month	Northern Hemisphere
4	Old Faithful geyser	Once every 35 to 120 minutes	1.5 to 5 minutes	Yellowstone National Park
5	Super bloom	Once a decade (though more often in recent years)	3 months	California's deserts
6	Total solar eclipse	Once every 18 months	Several hours	Worldwide

PSA: While decomposing leaves are integral to forest ecosystems, in suburbs across the country, this natural mulch and fertilizer is often bagged up in plastic and disposed of in landfills. According to the U.S. Environmental Protection Agency, leaves and other yard scraps account for more than 13 percent of the country's solid waste every year. When this occurs, the lack of oxygen halts the leaves' decomposition and instead causes them to release methane. Let the leaves fall where they may in your immediate surroundings, and you'll be supporting a tiny yet thriving community.

SEE GROWTH IN A NEW LIGHT

Growth as it applies to natural processes does not have the same definition that we think of in today's world of productivity, efficiency, and optimization. In a sense, their meanings are almost antithetical to each other. In the context of nature, healthy growth is measured by regeneration. In contemporary society, the most valued form of growth is one that comes from the constant betterment of oneself and one's output. So often, this growth is siloed and comes at the expense of other parts of ourselves. We value career over mind, image over body, individual over collective. Let's take a cue from nature and place greater value in the work that repeats, balances, and preserves.

PAY TRIBUTE TO THOSE WHO LEAF PEEPED HERE FIRST

It's no surprise fall colors have taken on much mythologizing throughout history, including in Native American folklore. An Iroquois legend tells of celestial hunters who, each fall, pursue a magical bear taunting their tribe. With the help of their dog, they're able to follow the bear's hidden tracks, which lead into the sky. They track it down at the end of the universe, and its slaying turns the forests below it red. As you're taking in the fall colors, recognize that they've long inspired and informed the original inhabitants of this land.

REMEMBER THERE ARE ALWAYS TWO SIDES TO EVERY STORY

J ust as the basis of *mono no aware* is the acceptance that there isn't life without death, take this time to explore the dichotomies that affect your outlook and, in turn, your well-being. When you think about what you've lost this past year, look up and remind yourself of the cyclical nature of life and of the beauty of impermanence. Take a walk and let the knowledge that our forests embrace winter rather than fight it be a reminder to embrace change and hardship, and to slow down and rest when you need to. Just as trees cast off their leaves when the effort outweighs the gain, shed the thoughts or things that don't serve you to make space for the clarity of winter and the new beginnings of spring.

Archetti, Marco. Richardson, Andrew D. O'Keefe, John. Delpierre, Nicolas. "Predicting Climate Change Impacts on the Amount and Duration of Autumn Colors in a New England Forest." Plos One, 2013. Retrieved via URL https://journals.plos.org/plosone/article?id=10.1371/journal.pone.0057373

Beckage, Brian. Osborne, Ben. Gavin, Daniel G. Pucko, Carolyn. Siccama, Thomas. Perkins, Timothy. "A rapid upward shift of a forest ecotone during 40 years of warming in the Green Mountains of Vermont." Proceedings of the National Academy of Sciences of the United States of America, 2008. Retrieved from URL https://www.pnas.org/content/105/11/4197

Brandon, Alice. "Tree and Shrub Identification Made Simple." Forest Preserves of Cook County, 2019.

Iyer, Pico. "Autumn Light: Season of Fire and Farewells." Knopf, 2019.

Koenig, John. "The Dictionary of Obscure Sorrows." Simon & Schuster, 2021.

Peters, M.P., Prasad, A.M., Matthews, S.N., & Iverson, L.R. 2020. Climate change tree atlas, Version 4. U.S. Forest Service, Northern Research Station and Northern Institute of Applied Climate Science, Delaware, OH. Retrieved via URL https://www.nrs.fs.fed.us/atlas

Shikibu, Murasaki. "The Tale of Genji (Penguin Classics Deluxe Edition)." Penguin Classics, 2002.

Smith, Charles W.G. "Fall Foliage: The Mystery, Science, and Folklore of Autumn Leaves." Falcon Guides, 2005.

Teika, Fujiwara. "Superior Poems of Our Time: A Thirteenth-Century Poetic Treatise and Sequence." Stanford University Press, 1967.

Thoreau, Henry David. "Autumnal Tints." *Atlantic*, 1862. Retrieved from URL https://www.theatlantic.com/magazine/archive/1862/10/autumnal-tints/308702/

Watts, Alan. "The Way of Zen." Vintage, 1999.